TWO BY TWO

TWO BY TWO

by

Steve English

solway

First published in 1998 by Solway

04 03 02 01 00 99 98   7 6 5 4 3 2 1

Solway in an imprint of Paternoster Publishing,
P.O. Box 300, Carlisle, Cumbria CA3 0QS, U.K.
http://www.paternoster-publishing.com

British Library Cataloguing in Publication Data
A catalogue record for this book is available from the British Library.

ISBN 1-900507-60-9

Cover design by Steve English
Typeset by WestKey Ltd, Falmouth, Cornwall
Printed in Great Britain by The Devonshire Press, Torquay

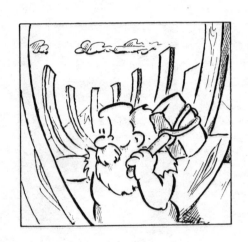

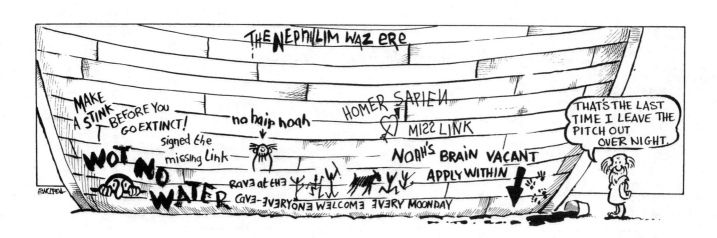

GOD TOLD NOAH AND
HIS FAMILY TO
TAKE TWO OF
EVERY LIVING
CREATURE INTO
THE ARK....

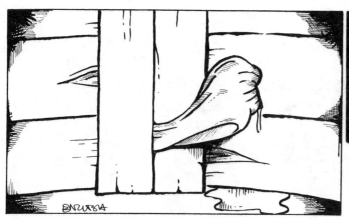

OF THE WHOLE OF HUMANITY, ONLY NOAH AND HIS WIFE, AND THEIR SONS WITH THEIR WIVES, WERE SAVED....

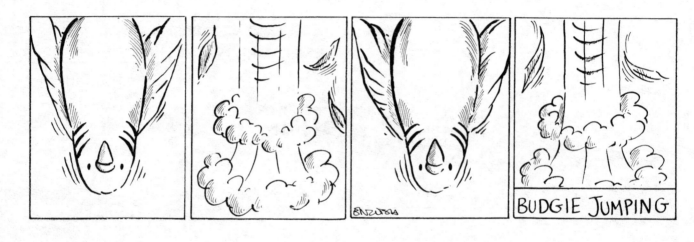

BUDGIE JUMPING

IN THE FEEDING FRENZY THE CATERPILLAR HAD MUNCHED HALF WAY THROUGH AN OLD FRIEND BEFORE EITHER OF THEM REALISED IT.

BURP

HEY, YOU'VE EATEN ONE OF MY WINGS! GERROFF!

IT'S YOUR FAULT FOR DISGUISING YOURSELF. HMMM, ACTUALLY YOU DON'T TASTE HALF BAD, CAN I HAVE ANOTHER NIBBLE?...

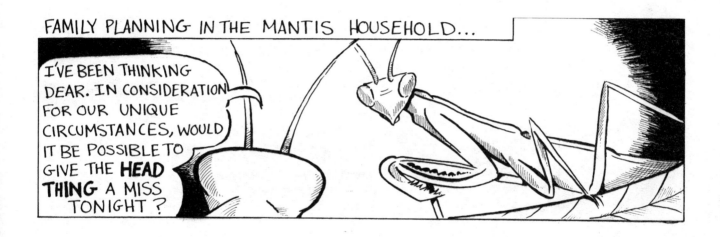

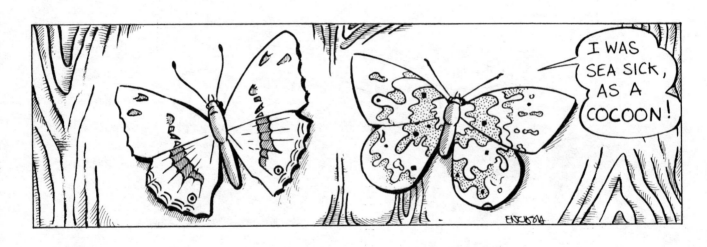

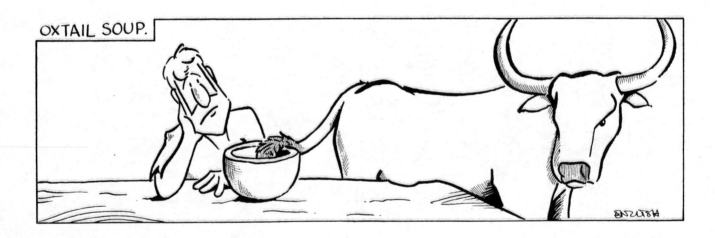

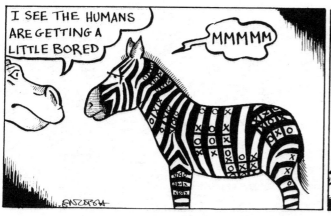

NOAH DECIDED HE WOULD HAVE TO CHOOSE THE BIRD THAT WAS TO BE SENT OUT OF THE ARK.

IT WAS A CASE OF THIRD TIME LUCKY FOR THE DOVE

AHHH, THIS IS COSY! NICE NEST EVEN IF I SAY SO MYSELF. NO WAY AM I GOING BACK TO THAT ARK.

SO WHAT SHALL I DO NOW.....?

HAVE ANOTHER BATH MAYBE!?

Peter's Cat

The disciple Peter is often featured in the New Testament but the observations and activities of his cat have not been recorded until now!

This light-hearted collection of cartoon illustrations provides a cat's-eye view, often comical, of many gospel passages combined with some alternative reflections from Proverbs.

Steve English, a free-lance illustrator, produced these cartoon strips for use in a student magazine but popular demand has resulted in their coming together in this witty compilation.

You will laugh as you enjoy this refreshingly tongue-in-cheek insight into the life of Peter's Cat.

"Peter's Cat sees some things that we could never see and thus there . . . are some quite different and unusual insights . . . striking, tongue-in-cheek and thought-provoking."
Ulster Christian

1-900507-17-X

solway